The MYTH, N

Feng Shui in Real Estate

How it Works and Why it Works... effortlessly

Suzee Miller

Feng Shui Author • Educator • Consultant

Produced by: AK Digital

This book is dedicated to my students and clients who, to this day, remain my greatest teachers.

Thank you for blessing my life with your passion and commitment to Feng Shui.

May you continue to grace and heal the environment, one property and one person at a time.

IN LOVING GRATITUDE,

Suzee Miller

Cover Design: Darko Angelovski
Illustrations: Jerry Wein
Edited: Gina Joly
Published: In the United States
Distributed: Worldwide
Produced by: AK Digital

CONTENTS

Your Free Feng Shui Element Profile

Each human-being comes into the world with "four" POWER directions.

Discover YOUR Personal Feng Shui element below to receive a FREE customized personality profile on your unique DNA.

Discovery Your Element at:

www.FengShuiBenefits.com/chiquiz

INTRODUCTION

In the late 90s, I was one of the corresponding journalists for the French TV station Canal + for the western half of the United States. Word travels fast about something good, and articles were popping up in France about Suzee Miller and how she uses Feng Shui to quickly turn listings. I was asked to do a report and come back with my findings.

The first meeting with Suzee was like every meeting with Suzee. She is the epitome of joy and delight and truly relishes the opportunity to help someone and share her amazing wisdom.

For the subject of our television report, she chose a house that had been listed for 2 years, the last 6 months of which had ZERO showings. The graveyard dance card was understandable. The house was located at a 'T' intersection. The couple had been living in the house and the wife got cancer and, after several terrible years during which the husband was dating her best friend, she killed herself in the master bedroom.

As you walked through the house, you could feel there was difficult energy. Even for someone like myself who, at the time, had little concept around 'feeling energy'… I could feel *that energy*!

Camera crew in place, Suzee with directions for all remedies in hand, we started the day at 10am and ended at 4pm. For these six hours, we had a crew implementing all the remedies as quickly as possible. This was a reality show before they even existed!

Some people were creating a little pond on the southwest side of the house as others were touching up the fence around the property. Others painting some walls terracotta red, others light golden yellow... gorgeous colors that gave a new personality to the house!

A statue here, a fountain there, a rug bringing a new splash of orange and warmth to the dining area. The house seemed to come alive! As I walked through the house with my camera crew filming the remedies as they were happening, I could feel a huge shift around me, but I could also see how it made me feel different on the inside too. I was fascinated by how such simple changes and additions made the house feel so different, transforming a simple house to a cozy home with elegance and intrigue.

As we reached the 4 o'clock hour, all the remedies complete, we all gathered in the living room to discuss the activities of the day. Suzee orchestrated the conversation, making sure everything on her list had been addressed. Satisfied with the success of the day, it was time for a closing prayer. With great reverence and respect, Suzee lit a bowl of alcohol and Epsom salt and delivered a loving prayer over each one of us, the house, each part of the house, and each inhabitant and experience that had ever happened in the house.

It was a prayer that was very intentional and directly guided. With the flames flickering in a captivating dance, Suzee's words guided our minds through the rooms as she blessed each part. These were all so familiar to us as we had been working very hard there all day. This final blessing had a very powerful impact and sense of completion. With what happened next, I could not believe my eyes!

Suddenly, as Suzee was finishing the prayer, a woman came up to the house and knocked on the window where we were praying. She was wanting to know if she could see the house! Me and my crew were shocked. But Suzee had a knowing smile. She's seen this many, many times before.

Three days later, the house SOLD for $5,000 over the list price with two back-up offers!

When it comes to this kind of phenomenon, it's hard to really pinpoint the real reason. Is it luck? Is it just a coincidence that the house sold right away? Maybe it was going to sell anyway... I mean, isn't it just a matter of time? This experience surprised me but was quickly forgotten.

My editor was very happy with the report, so I went back to daily life. I forgot about it until one day, I heard back from Suzee. We discussed the segment and footage, and I got a copy of the report to her.

As I handed a copy of the TV show over to Suzee, she looked me in the eye and said, "You're still not a believer! I can tell." To which I honestly replied, "It was a great story! And I was really fascinated by the fact that the house sold so fast. But it could be coincidence."

My frankness washed over Suzee, and with her ever-present, joyful exuberance and a challenging look in her eye, she said, "I'm going to make a believer out of you yet! I'm going to Feng Shui

your house! NO CHARGE – MY GIFT TO YOU. I want you to see on a personal level what Feng Shui really does!"

With nothing to lose, I promptly agreed. Now, I had been shocked when the woman showed up at the window during Suzee's prayer at the house for the report. That was truly a shocking moment! But that was nothing compared to Suzee's analysis of my home! As we walked through each room, she could tell me intricate facts about my life that some of my closest friends didn't even know! From the doors of the bedroom not closing and their direction, she could tell there was discord on a very deep level in my personal relationship and possibly already a divorce.

She was right! My marriage of 12 years was agonizingly falling apart, and the divorce was 'in process.' That coupled with other mathematic equations for other rooms delivered even more deep dark secrets that emerged as indirect questions from her lips. I couldn't believe the facts she could gather from compass directions of the house, construction and remodel years and my birth date. It was absolutely mind-blowing how accurate it all was!

At one point, I said to Suzee in disbelief,

"How is it possible you can know these deep secrets about me from such little information?!" Suzee's response was to the point "The Chinese have perfected many sciences that have been around for thousands of years. As the science of the meridians and Chinese medicine apply and are very successful for the body, so does Feng Shui apply to the energy flows of the house. That too is an organism. A house is an organism. Our mother earth is an organism. All is a living organism!"

At the conclusion of our consultation, Suzee gave me several remedies. They were mostly simple remedies with one complicated remedy. I had to quit using the front door and turn the garden door into the new front door as the floor plan of the house had initially intended. I had fun getting a new creative door made and took 3 weeks to get it all in place.

Then… the magic started! Although I was still very sad to see the end of my marriage, my whole life started shifting. My job where I worked with my ex-husband's close friends suddenly changed. They decided to close the LA office and sent me off to Europe to make plans for my future.

With many great options on the table, and me the indecisive buyer, they told me that they would continue to pay my salary for the next 5 months while I 'thought about it.' I could go on vacation and enjoy thinking …. slowly! I enjoyed Europe as never before and was cradled as the only American on the island of Stromboli during the heart-breaking tragedy of September 11th. A very safe and reassuring place to be.

Upon my return to the United States, I decided on the severance package that delivered over $70,000 to my bank account and the wherewithal to start a new life.

Now again, is this coincidence or is there really something to Feng Shui? To answer that question, you'll have to decide for yourself. As for me, I am a believer!

Gina Joly

International Freelance Journalist

Author's Message

Dearest Reader,

Are you ready to step outside the box of the mundane and start living an outrageously ABUNDANT and JOY FILLED life?

If so, it is my passion and pleasure to help you optimize and harmonize your property so that it is at its highest potential. It's at this point of BALANCE that your environment (or real estate listing) will "effortlessly" attract the right relationships and/or the right buyers who would benefit the most from such a home or property.

This book is NOT about "how to" Feng Shui.

It's about how to set the FOUNDATION for "good" Feng Shui to MANIFEST so that you can enjoy "seen and unseen" BENEFITS AND MIRACLES beyond your imagination.

What I do is not about sales, although it's a fantastic secondary benefit.

What I seek is HARMONY.

To Enable it, to Promote it, and to Share it.

So that you can become the CREATOR of your own destiny, and not someone else's.

In this Feng Shui book, I will share with you some insights I've gathered over the years, and give you a birds-eye view into what Feng Shui IS and what it can do for you.

As a real estate broker for 30+ years, I have experienced the ebb and flow of the marketplace, but it was not until the day I learned about Feng Shui that my life and career changed forever.

I first learned western Feng Shui and applied some of the principles to "unsellable" properties. Then, I went on to learn other schools of Feng Shui which greatly increased the marketability of real estate listings.

I was fascinated with what the different schools and approaches of Feng Shui had in common, but even more so by how they differed. Those differences made it CLEAR to me that the "essential elements" of Feng Shui need to be given MACRO attention.

Hence, to achieve BRILLIANT SUCCESS with this ancient modality, there are THREE CORE PRINCIPLES that are essential and that must, therefore, be applied correctly.

Sadly, these principles are often misunderstood or overlooked altogether in the mad dash to make things "look pretty."

I hope that my approach to Feng Shui and how to apply it to your home, office and/or property listings will help you achieve extraordinary SUCCESS AND HAPPINESS, like it has done for thousands of my students and clients worldwide.

I have INTENTIONALLY written this book in short and simple paragraphs, and have inserted bold sentences and CAPITALIZED words that are important for you to focus on and remember. I have also added WHITE SPACE to encourage you to pause and reflect. Hopefully, this will also help you learn a complex study with the least amount of effort.

My life's mission is to TRANSFORM LIVES by educating people on the INFINITE possibilities that "vibrant and balanced" ENERGY provides. The teaching, consulting, and sharing of Feng Shui has been my life's purpose, and it is my honor and privilege to share my INTEGRATIVE approach with you.

May your journey into Feng Shui grace your life and those that you encounter along the way.

IN JOY,

Suzee Miller

Chapter One

Do YOU Believe in MIRACLES?

I know we all want to believe in miracles, but in truth, are they real?

What if creating miracles isn't something that requires years of spiritual training or alchemy?

I believe creating MIRACLES is our natural birthright.

In my experience with Feng Shui, creating miracles is as easy and natural as breathing.

Therefore, wherever you find yourself in life today, know that your situation is simply your personal "myth and mind-set," and that if you desire a richer, healthier, happier and/or less stressful life, you can change everything with the ancient wisdom that Feng Shui provides.

The very reason you are here on earth is to work through your "perceived" challenges, dramas, and dilemmas through the realization of your own power.

Self-knowledge leading to self-mastery is the ultimate quest, the pivotal adventure of a lifetime.

With Feng Shui skill and knowledge, you can start living your aspirations and dreams now, rather than at some unforeseeable time in the future.

As you progress through this book, you will discover "countless" benefits that Feng Shui can bring to your life. However, there are NINE specific **MIRACLES** that will occur MAGICALLY *when you are ready to hold yourself and your environment accountable and responsible for your life and destiny*.

This translates to experiencing an AWAKENING, one which allows you to live your life with focused INTENTION AND ATTENTION in the NOW.

I am sure there are more than NINE Feng Shui Miracles, but here are the most obvious ones:

1. YOUR FENG SHUI ELEMENT.

Everyone has a personal Feng Shui Element. Knowing yours helps you to understand some of your tendencies and natural affinities. This is what I refer to as your personal DNA.

Enhancing your environment to compliment your "unique" element helps to magnify your highest potential. This knowledge will benefit and enrich all the areas of your life, including, but not limited to, your health, sleep, relationships, wealth, love, peace of mind and good fortune.

This school of Feng Shui, called EIGHT MANSIONS or BA-ZHAI ("Baa Sigh"), has created more Millionaires, Billionaires, and HAPPY people than all the other schools combined (more on this will be given to you as you proceed).

2. MINDFULLNESS

Feng Shui is a wonderful way to bring consciousness to everything in your environment.

In other words, you will naturally become more mindful when you fully integrate Feng Shui principles into your life.

This means multiple things. Not only will YOU be more knowledgeable and understanding of your true self (or higher self), but it also means that you will be more MINDFUL of your surroundings and those of others. This alone will help to calm your nerves, sharpen your senses, and enhance your reflexes and mental agility.

Without effort, you will become a more POSITIVE person because your home and/or working environment supports you.

When you are mindful and focused in the NOW, it's simply impossible to live yesterday's story or be fearful of tomorrow.

3. GOALS

Everyone has goals in life; however, Feng Shui helps you identify yours and reach them faster.

With proper placement (arrangement of your furnishing) and incorporating the THREE CORE PRINCIPLES OF FENG SHUI, you will be able to control and direct the energy in your home and office to specific locations within your environment. This will automatically boost your INTENTION AND ATTENTION towards achieving your goals.

Keep in mind that with Feng Shui, YOU ARE YOUR ENVIRONMENT, and because there is no separation between you and it, you will start to live a life filled with infinite possibilities and opportunities.

No longer will you feel the need to escape or seek out places better than your own. Harmony, peace, and balance will become the REALITY of your creation – your environment, your SPACE.

4. HABITS

Once you have removed clutter and disarray from your environment and have implemented the core principles of Feng Shui, you will find that it is far easier to break bad habits.

By eliminating bad habits, you will be FOCUSED on achieving your visions, dreams, and goals in the present moment.

You will discover that living life in the PRESENT MOMENT is safe and easier with Feng Shui.

5. CONNECTION

As you begin to feel more harmonious with your environment, so too will you feel more connected with nature and mankind.

Almost magically, new people, places and opportunities will reveal themselves to you, and you will begin to feel a new level of

GRATITUDE and THANKSGIVING beyond the depths of anything you have experienced before.

Love will vanquish every negative thought and judgment you hold in consciousness.

6. ENERGY

The only way you can become more engaged with the world, in the first place, is if you have the energy to do so.

Feng Shui is the "life force energy" that revitalizes your mind, body, spirit and soul.

An energetically BALANCED environment not only supports positive thinking and being, but it also supports MIRACLES.

7. ABUNDANCE

When Feng Shui is practiced correctly, it creates pathways to INFINITE possibilities, opportunities, and good fortune.

Abundance comes in many forms. It can be in the way of money, vibrant health, a fulfilling sex life, restful sleep, improved communication, clarity, and authenticity in all relationships - especially the one with yourself.

It's a simple fact. GOOD Feng Shui is a beacon of POSITIVE ENERGY that magnetizes and attracts ABUNDANCE and BLESSINGS, naturally.

8. CREATIVITY

When you live in a HARMONICALLY balanced environment (which you will learn about later), your creative juices will flow naturally and abundantly.

When the energy around you flows freely, your CONSCIOUSNESS EXPANDS beyond the visible plane, and you start living a fulfilling life without anxiety, fear, or worry.

It's an amazing phenomenon, but with Feng Shui, the universe (or God) constantly supports and fuels your CREATIVE intelligence. This is an indescribable gift (blessing) that Feng Shui brings to your life.

9. PASSION

To live life FULLY EXPRESSED is the greatest gift you can give yourself. This means living and communicating the TRUTH, no matter the outcome.

Feng Shui encourages you to take risks, to explore new territory, and to take quantum leaps in growth, while committing yourself to your highest level of evolution and happiness.

This ancient art and science empowers you to hold yourself accountable and responsible for your role in everything.

In other words, to live your life CONSCIOUSLY and COURAGEOUSLY in every moment.

When YOU and your environment are in alignment, you will realize how POWERFUL you are, and nothing will ever stop you (again) from living YOUR life PASSIONATELY.

Feng Shui removes the veil – to the perceived obstacles in your path - that holds you back from living life LARGE, and from experiencing MIRACLES as your natural birthright.

It also helps you to see that "everything" that IS OR ISN'T happening in your life is either a LESSON or BLESSING … or both.

Chapter Two

What Feng Shui IS and What It IS NOT

Feng Shui is the study of ENERGY and how energy "impacts" BUILDINGS, LAND, AND PEOPLE.

Feng Shui IS NOT about philosophy, religion, superstition, nor is it an occult practice.

The goal of GOOD Feng Shui is to regulate the flow and accumulation of POSITIVE Life Force ENERGY.

When this is accomplished – TIME, SPACE, PEOPLE, AND THE ENVIRONMENT UNITE AS ONE INTEGRAL ENTITY to attract opportunities, blessings, and good fortune... *effortlessly.*

A good Feng Shui environment promotes peace, balance, harmonious relations, vitality, health, love, conception, wealth, and unbound creativity.

In truth, it is impossible to name all the BENEFITS Feng Shui can bring to your life and career in just one book, but if you are interested – here are a few benefits of importance: Fengshuibenefits.com/benefits

ADDITIONAL **BENEFITS** will be given to you throughout the book as well.

For now, here is what you need to know.

FENG SHUI is an application of art and science.

The "art of placement" is what most people are familiar with and consider to be Feng Shui. It is the placement and arrangement of material items to help create harmonious flow. However, this is just a fraction of what the true art of Feng Shui is about.

From a scientific perspective, classical Feng Shui is the study of organic and inorganic matter.

The Chinese call this "Wu Li."

In our Western culture, we refer to Wu Li as Quantum Mechanics or Quantum Physics.

Feng Shui (pronounced fung schway), literally translated, means WIND AND WATER. It refers to our environment - that piece of land, that portion of the earth that was shaped by the power of wind and water. Our earth's size, shape, topography, and its overall appearance is continually changing and being transformed by these two forces of nature.

Feng Shui is often described in the following Chinese phrase:

"Tian ling di li ren he," which means auspicious heavenly influence, beneficial topography, harmonious human action, and balanced environment.

Everything in the universe is comprised of energy. The way energy flows in through and around your environment dynamically affects your life and career.

The Chinese call this energy CHI (Qi).

Feng Shui has been practiced since the Tang Dynasty (618-907 A.D.) Its founder, Master Yan Yun-Sang, was the principle advisor to the court of Emperor Hi Tsang.

Until recently, this literature on Feng Shui was not available in English.

The art of Feng Shui is rich in symbolism, and the science of Feng Shui is based on invisible energies, both of which contribute to the cultural barrier between the East and West.

In the East, the focus is to live in harmony with nature, whereas in the West, we try to control or harness nature to make it work to our benefit.

Modern Day Application:

Today, Feng Shui is increasingly utilized by architects, city planners, landscape designers, interior decorators, stagers, real estate agents, business executives and homeowners to create BALANCED environments.

A balanced environment creates "symphonic harmony" that exudes GRACE, PEACE AND BEAUTY.

Chapter Three

Feng Shui Rates Number THREE

Surprisingly, Feng Shui is not the most important consideration to the Chinese people who introduced the world to Feng Shui. Later in this book, you will understand more of the reasons why it's number three.

For now, here is what you need to know.

There are FIVE METAPHYSICAL ABSTRACTS the Chinese consider imperative to the creation of a balanced life for a human-being. Here they are in their order of importance:

#1 ~ DESTINY

The Chinese believe that your destiny is governed by the time, day & year of your birth.

The solar system rules in the destiny of one's life, and it is the number one important factor in the fate of mankind.

#2 ~ LUCK

You may find it hard to believe, but LUCK is a very strong Chinese concept. They believe that luck may or may not accompany you throughout your lifetime.

Luck may bless you at your birthplace or by the family you were born into. Likewise, the choices you make during your life can also influence and affect your good fortune.

#3 ~ FENG SHUI

The Chinese fascination with luck is what erroneously makes people believe that Feng Shui is steeped in superstition.

This is a MYTH.

Feng Shui is not about superstition, it is not about religion, and it is not about philosophy. It is about living in HARMONY with mother earth and the environment.

The reality is that the fate of humanity can be enhanced and changed dramatically by the two forces of nature that govern the essence of Feng Shui.

WIND AND WATER.

#4 ~ PHILANTHROPY AND CHARITY

The Chinese believe that what you do with your money is a way of recycling GOODNESS back into Earth's luck and energy.
They also believe that if you honor the forces in nature, nature will honor you with abundant wealth, vibrant health, and good fortune.

Equally important is giving back to others. It is another great way of spreading good ENERGY.

#5 ~ EDUCATION AND SELF DEVELOPMENT

What one does with one's mind, is very important to the Chinese. Additionally, it is a way of assuring that positive energy and good fortune will BLESS your life.

Now, you may be wondering why "philanthropy and charity" and "education & self-development," are at the bottom of the list.

Chinese Masters practice the philosophy that we are ONE WITH NATURE, and that when we live in HARMONY with nature, nature will honor us...infinitely.

They believe that if their properties, their homes, their offices, even their cars and parking lots have good Feng Shui, it will enhance their luck, their fortune and even their destiny. AND, when this is accomplished, philanthropy, charity, education & self-development are a given.

Likewise, Feng Shui may rate #3 in order of importance (which seems low), but there is a significance to this positioning. The number THREE equates to BLESSINGS.

Therefore, "good" Feng Shui has the ability to manifest HUMAN RIGHT ACTION.

By getting yourself in harmony and balance with the flow of nature's energy – or with what I refer to as *the STREAM OF GRACE* – the Chinese believe that YOU can change your destiny and fortune forever.

AND, the truth IS that I've been blessed to witness this MIRACLE countless times.

Chapter Four

MASTERING Feng Shui

Feng Shui is not difficult to learn, but there is certainly more to it than meets the hand and eye.

This is the reason it is important for you to MASTER Feng Shui.

AND, the good news is .. YOU CAN DO IT.

A Feng Shui Master is a composer of natural energies.

He or she has a direct effect on our lives, on our physical and emotional health, intellect, moods, perceptions and even our view points.

These energies already exist in nature and are in harmony where nature exists by itself.

As humans, we have evolved and learned to modify our surroundings. This has had a direct impact on the energies of our environment, and in most cases, it has created extreme discord.

Each place we occupy, whether it be a room, office, home, building or park, has many seen and unseen energies that affect us, short or long term.

Using the "natural energies" of an environment to its most POSITIVE POTENTIAL is what Feng Shui is about.

FOR EXAMPLE:

Imagine entering a concert hall where the musicians are playing their instruments randomly at varying intensities and durations.

No matter how wonderfully skilled each individual musician is, the result would still be chaotic discord. It would not take long before the "noise" (SHA CHI) would be so irritating it would begin to create "negative" emotions and energy.

Thus, in the same way a composer of a symphony creates auditory magnificence from the direct arrangement of each musician, instrument and musical note, a Master of Feng Shui compositions creates magnificent harmony from chaotic and discordant energies around us.

When Feng Shui is orchestrated correctly, it creates a HARMONIC SYMPHONY of energy that binds the Universe and all life together.

Good Feng Shui is the flow of vibrant and balanced energy that feels MYSTICAL, MAGICAL, AND GLORIOUS in every conceivable and inconceivable way.

The flow of HARMONIC ENERGY unlocks our hearts and souls to the infinite possibilities, opportunities and blessings that exist in life. It also gives us the courage to stretch ourselves (the story we tell ourselves about who we are) to the maximum.

This is a Feng Shui REALITY.

Chapter Five

See MORE - Have MORE – Be MORE

If you were asked what specifically comes to mind when you think of your house or office, what would your first thought BE?

Maybe you would think of how relaxed you feel thanks to how organized your SPACE is today. Or, perhaps you might think about how much you enjoy your garden or the view from your window.

Regardless of the thoughts that come to mind, what's important is that they be POSITIVE.

Whether positive to you means being at peace, relaxed, joyful, happy, or inspired, an environment that makes you feel or think positive thoughts and emotions will be a place that you ultimately enjoy occupying.

IN TRUTH – YOU ARE YOUR ENVIRONMENT, AS THERE IS NO SEPARATION IN ENERGY.

Feng Shui is a unique modality designed to create harmony, peace, and balance in SPATIAL ENVIRONMENTS, be it your home, office, landscape, office, or real estate listings.

The extraordinary benefits of Feng Shui can be felt almost immediately after you activate the THREE CORE PRINCIPLES of this art and science.

This is another Feng Shui REALITY.

Throughout the book, we will explore what Feng Shui IS and what Feng Shui is NOT.

Sadly, too many books and websites on the subject confuse the superstitions and cultural beliefs of the Chinese people with the true art and science of Feng Shui.

Good Feng Shui is LIMITLESS once you learn the CORE PRINCIPLES. You can practice them on your home, garden, office, desk, computer and even on something as small as your business card.

As you go about your day-to-day life, your environment is constantly communicating with you.

It's simple. If you wish to live a more positive life, then it's important to become aware and conscious of the influences you're receiving, every moment, from your environment and learn how to manage them.

Feng Shui is about living life ... CONSCIOUSLY.

It's about being MINDFUL of your environment and bringing it into harmony and balance so that your body, mind, and spirit are supported in rich and miraculous ways.

In this book, you will be provided with a thorough introduction to Feng Shui, how it originated, what it's about, and how you can apply the THREE CORE PRINCIPLES to your environment.

Chapter Six

Core Principle Number ONE

There are several goals to achieve with Feng Shui. However, the ULTIMATE GOAL of Feng Shui *IS to…*

UNITE Time, People, Space, and the Environment as ONE INTEGRAL ENTITY, so that Heaven, Earth, and Human Beings are in HARMONY AND BALANCE.

To accomplish this, it's important to understand the THREE CORE principles of Feng Shui, as they originate in concept from the beginning of time.

The ancient philosophy known as TAOISM or the TAO (pronounced dow) means THE WAY or the natural flow of the Universe. It is sometimes referred to as Daoism as well.

Lao Tzu or Laozi, who existed in 6th century B.C, was the founder of the Chinese philosophy or the 'School of the Tao' or 'Taoism.'

The TAO comprises everything in the universe.

It is the Chinese explanation of life and the existence of Heaven, Earth, and Mankind.

In terms of Feng Shui, the TAO divides the Universe into two primal forces which make up the FIRST CORE PRINCIPLE of Feng Shui.

The YIN/YANG Theory – Core Principle Number ONE

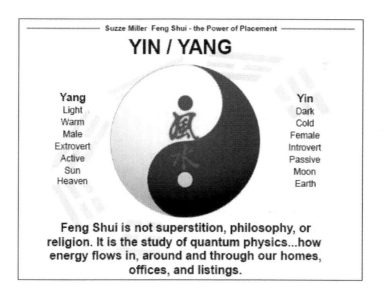

YIN AND YANG are opposites:

Yin and Yang complement each other to form a balanced environment.

As polarities, one cannot exist without the other.

The Yin/Yang symbol is a circular ball in space, half black - half white.

Inside the black half is a dot of white, and inside the white half, there is a dot of black.

Each has the essence of the other in them, symbolic of the fact that Yin/Yang cannot exist without each other.

Yin and Yang each have their proper place in your life.

The coziness of a mountain cabin is a perfect example of a YIN environment.

A place to curl up and retreat from the maddening world.

A Yang environment is typically light, bright, open, and airy. It makes for a great work station.

A Yang environment is a great place to meet people.

The beach is the best example of a Yang environment. The sun on the sand on a beautiful day is a perfect example of Yang energy.

One of the aims of Feng Shui is to achieve a BALANCE in characteristics that oppose one another in the world around you. According to the theory of Yin/Yang, everything in the universe consists of forces that are interconnected and yet opposing one another.

YIN IS FEMININE ENERGY, AND YANG IS MASCULINE ENERGY.

Yin is soft, passive, and nurturing, while Yang is hard, active, and aggressive.

If you look around, you will see Yin and Yang opposites in your daily life, such as hot and cold temperatures, soft and hard furnishings, a dark and light room, and so on. Yin and Yang exist everywhere in our homes, in office buildings, and in nature as well.

It is the interaction between these two opposing forces

YIN/YANG

that create HARMONY around you.

It is very easy to balance Yin/Yang in your home.

You can add soft cushions to wooden chairs or cold bathwater to hot bathwater to balance the temperatures. You can paint one side of the room a dark color and the other side a lighter color.

When Yin and Yang are in balance with one another, you will always feel more at peace and more comfortable.

Yin energy is represented by the colors black, blue and deep purple. Outdoors in nature, it is the element WATER.

Yin is the energy that you use at night when you want sleep or when you need to relax during the day. It is the energy of silence and darkness.

Yang energy colors are white, gold, and silver. It is represented by the element METAL in nature.

It is a strong energy that is always in motion; it's the energy you use when working at the office or spending time with your family or being outdoors.

The Yin/Yang Theory of balance is even more critical when you're in an environment with poor Feng Shui conditions.

An example of such an environment would be a (typical) office, packed with computers, hard floors, metal cabinets, ringing phones, and wooden desks which result in feelings of irritation, stress, and even isolation.

It is extremely difficult to be productive or creative in this type of "chaotic" environment.

By adding more YIN ENERGY to this office scenario, it would help to balance the environment.

Yin items would be such things as soft fabrics, wooden file cabinets instead of metal, calming colors or artwork on the walls and perhaps some soothing background music as well.

The important thing to understand about the YIN/YANG THEORY is the concept of BALANCE.

Balance harmonizes an environment and allows energy to flow effortlessly. When energy flows effortlessly and gently, it nurtures and supports you mentally, emotionally, and spiritually.

Chapter Seven

The TAO and Feng Shui

What exactly is the TAO, and more importantly, what does it have to do with Feng Shui?

Feng Shui and Taoism, in general, share very similar philosophies, including the universal energy CHI (Qi) that is expressed in numerous forms.

The 'Tao' simply means the 'way' or the 'path.'

It cannot be truly described in words, because as humans we are far removed from its actual essence. Instead, it must be "felt" to be understood.

Feng Shui and Taoism share many of the same disciplines, as they both seek ways for humans to align with the harmony found in nature.

The epitome of the Tao is 'going with the flow.'

When energy is flowing, you can make major leaps forward in your life. Conversely, when energy slows down, it allows your body to feel more relaxed and peaceful.

In its essence, Taoism is about how the WISDOM of the universe carries you to your goals and allows you to achieve what you desire without undue stress or effort.

A Chinese Master once shared with me an interesting perspective on ENERGY and the Tao.

To paraphrase him, he said that at birth each human being is granted a defined quantity of energy to utilize during their lifetime. How we choose to use this energy is up to us. However, Feng Shui allows us to make each second of ENERGY in our lives count with the least amount of effort.

In other words, Feng Shui principles and techniques provide you a way to achieve anything that your heart desires with ease and grace, so that your "precious time" on earth is not wasted.

A key principle of the Tao and Feng Shui, as you learned in the last chapter, is the principle of the YIN/YANG THEORY, or the study of the two opposing forces of the universe. Every Feng Shui school, including both classical schools and western schools, revolve around how one can create a harmonious balance of energy.

The YIN/YANG Theory is at the very heart of Feng Shui, and is the FIRST CORE PRINCIPLE of this ancient art and science.

Yet, Taoism and Feng Shui are not entirely the same because Feng Shui has evolved into a direction that is separate from the Tao.

In fact, Feng Shui is an offshoot of the Tao.

Taoism (also known as Daoism or the Dao) focuses on "action through inaction" and the easiest way to accomplish things, whereas Feng Shui is the study of environments that align with universal energies which nurture and support you.

Nonetheless, the roots of Taoism are still ingrained very strongly in Feng Shui, which is why understanding Taoism is key to understanding Feng Shui.

When you align yourself with how energy feels at any given moment, which Taoism is about, then you can also create good Feng Shui.

Learning how to recognize energy is not complex. You simply sense it and flow with it, rather than resist it.

Chapter Eight

Core Principle Number TWO

As the Tao unfolds, Yin/Yang expresses itself in the universe through the forces of nature called THE FIVE CHINESE ELEMENTS.

This is core principle number TWO.

The FIVE elements are: FIRE, EARTH, METAL, WATER, and WOOD.

The interaction of the FIVE CHINESE ELEMENTS determines whether an environment is in BALANCE or not.

This is where learning Feng Shui starts to get a bit more complex, as there are "three cycles" to the FIVE ELEMENTS that are important for you to understand and utilize.

In the study of the five elements, the Chinese honor the POWER of the elements by observing how the elements work in relationship to each other.

The THREE CYCLES OF ENERGY (or five elements) are called the: PRODUCTIVE, REDUCTIVE and DESTRUCTIVE cycles.

Please refer to the graph below.

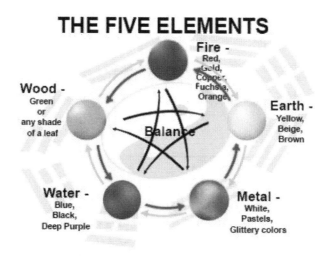

The PRODUCTIVE Cycle of ELEMENTS represents radiant energy. (Note the direction of the outer arrow.)

It is the natural flow of EASE, GRACE, AND ABUNDANCE. It is energy that feels good and flows effortlessly, and it is aesthetically "beautiful" because it is in BALANCE. The intertwining of these elements becomes a beautiful dance, a symphony of the senses that creates HARMONY.

The REDUCTIVE Cycle of ENERGY is used to "soften" the effects of a specific element, or to reduce or slow down energy – an imbalance - of one or more elements. (Note the direction of the inner arrow.)

The DESTRUCTIVE cycle is used to cancel out "chaotic" energy altogether. (Note the star in the center of the diagram above.)

Each cycle is distinctive and different, but their rhythms can be used to your Feng Shui advantage, as each cycle can be used as medicine to remedy, correct or improve an environment.

Let's take a deeper dive into the FIVE ELEMENTS and their cycles.

THE PRODUCTIVE CYCLE OF THE FIVE ELEMENTS

Good Feng Shui is reflected in the **Productive Cycle**, where each element produces the next element in the cycle.

Here's how it works:

Note the diagram with a circle of five floating balls rotating in a CLOCKWISE motion.

At the very top of the circle is the element FIRE. If you think about it, the element Fire snaps, crackles, and pops, and when it dies out, it creates ash.

Ash becomes the next element, EARTH.

Earth, in a productive cycle, creates all the ores or the next element, METAL.

Metal in a vapor or liquid state acts like the next element, WATER.

Water, the dynamic of water, feeds the element, WOOD.

Wood then becomes fuel for FIRE...

Here is a recap of the PRODUCTIVE CYCLE OF ELEMENTS:

Fire creates Earth (Ash)

Earth creates Metal (Ores/Minerals)

Metal becomes Water (Vapor/Liquid)

Water nurtures Wood (Plants/Trees)

Wood fuels Fire (Flames)

THE REDUCTIVE CYCLE OF THE FIVE ELEMENTS

It's not as confusing as it may seem to identify cycles, as you can feel the energy of the elements in an environment. All you need to do is quiet your mind and observe the energy.

FOR EXAMPLE:

You may even be able to remember a time when you walked into a gorgeous hotel lobby and felt totally embraced by the environment.

The five Chinese elements were in a productive cycle. They created a balanced environment. It was the equal ratio of each element, "visually," that made you feel comfortable/good.

When this happens, an environment supports, nurtures, and enriches your life.

HOWEVER, the opposite is true of an out-of-balance environment; it affects you differently.

FOR EXAMPLE:

It is when you walk into a room and feel uncomfortable. You may even have the urge to get out.

What is happening is that you are ENERGETICALLY feeling the effects of an out-of-balance environment.

Referring again to the five floating balls, imagine reversing the direction COUNTER-CLOCKWISE now, to REDUCE or correct the imbalance that is present.

FOR EXAMPLE:

If there was too much green (the wood element) present in a room, you would want to add the FIRE element to reduce (slow down) the radiating energy of the wood element.

In this scenario, FIRE BURNS WOOD; therefore, fire would burn off the over dominant wood present in the room. By simply adding a RED décor item to the room, you would be able to bring the room (environment) back into balance.

A recap of the REDUCTIVE CYCLE and how it works:

FIRE REDUCES WOOD

WOOD SUCKS-UP WATER

WATER CORRODES METAL

METAL DEPLETES THE EARTH

EARTH PUTS OUT FIRE

Thus, using the REDUCTIVE CYCLE, or the counter clockwise rotation of the ELEMENTS, you can reduce the over dominant element or elements that are out of balance.

THE DESTRUCTIVE CYCLE OF ELEMENTS

You will want to use the DESTRUCTIVE cycle of elements when an environment is WAY OUT OF BALANCE.

It represents an environment where one or more of the elements OVERWHELM space. AND, because you are your environment or the space you occupy– it also depletes your body energy.

FOR EXAMPLE:

If you walked into a bedroom and saw 5 green plants, a green bedspread, green drapes and a green carpet, the element Wood would "visually and energetically" DOMINATE the environment.

Likewise, when an element overwhelms space, it also drains the other elements, and harmony and balance cannot be sustained. To remedy this imbalance, use the DESTRUCTIVE cycle of elements.

Once again referring to the five floating balls, this time look at the FIVE POINT STAR that has been formed to show you how to DESTROY an over-dominant element.

Here is how the DESTRUCTIVE Cycle works:

FIRE MELTS METAL

METAL CHOPS WOOD

WOOD SUCKS THE NUTRIENTS FROM THE EARTH

EARTH DAMS WATER

WATER PUTS FIRE OUT

Chapter Nine

Which Cycle to Use, and WHEN

How do you KNOW when the elements are in a productive cycle, and how do you know when to use the Reductive cycle or a Destructive cycle to remedy an environment?

In Western Feng Shui, you need only to OBSERVE the environment to see if the five elements are present and in balance (in close to equal ratios), or if they are not.

When one or more elements dominate an environment, the environment becomes SHA - out of balance energy - and requires the use of the Reductive or Destructive cycles to remedy it.

The elements can also be out of balance when one or more elements are "missing" in an environment; this, too, can cause imbalance. Thus, you will need to decide how to remedy an out-of-balance environment and when to either add a missing element (or two) or reduce or destroy one or more elements.

I know the THREE CYCLES of the element can get confusing, but fortunately, God gave you INTUITION, and this is the perfect time to trust your inner knowing and use it.

Here are a few TIPS to help you develop your intuition in Feng Shui:

Act like a third-party inspector and scan each room in your home or real estate listing for the FIVE ELEMENTS.

Ask yourself if one or more elements are over dominant or missing in the environment.

If it is "really obvious" to you that an element is OVER DOMINANT in a room– use the Destructive cycle to remedy it. Do the same for other elements present in the room that may be over dominant as well.

If you "feel" a room just needs to be "tweaked a bit" to balance the five elements, use the Reductive Cycle to remedy the imbalance.

If you discover there is a MISSING element, then add a décor item or a color that represents the missing element to bring the environment into balance.

TRUST that if a room "feels good" and all the elements are present in close to equal ratios, then you need not do anything.

Chapter Ten

The Chinese ELEMENTS

I could write an entire book just on THE FIVE CHINESE ELEMENTS and how powerful they are individually and collectively.

TOO, I can honestly say that I am shocked by the environments that I see on a regular basis.

Rarely do I see an ELEMENTALLY BALANCED home, office, or real estate listing. Usually, they are over dominant in one or more elements, which throws the remaining elements out of balance.

Not only is this BAD Feng Shui, but it can also wreak major havoc on the lives of the occupants who work or live in these spaces.

Therefore, it's important for you to learn HOW and WHEN to use the elements to create harmony and balance – GOOD Feng Shui.

Below are different aspects of the FIVE ELEMENTS.

The FIVE ELEMENTS are associated with several things. Knowing them allows you to use additional "techniques" to bring an environment into balance – VISUALLY.

They are:

> Directions
>
> Seasons

Colors

Symbols

Shapes

Here is what you need to know about each element:

The element FIRE

Fire represents the direction SOUTH on the Compass.

Season: SUMMER

Color: RED, Fuchsia, Orange, Gold, Copper, Sunflower Gold

This element can be substituted with a lamp or light, a candle or color.

Shape: TRIANGLE, pyramid, or anything pointed or jagged

A house or structure with sharp lines and angles is considered a fire building.

The element EARTH

Radiates to the directions of NORTHEAST AND SOUTHWEST

Earth is BETWEEN seasons.

Color: Soft YELLOW, Beige, Off White, any Soft Earth tone color

Element substitution: Crystal, STONE floors and counter tops, pottery

Shape: SQUARE or rectangular (not circular or round like our earth)

A square or rectangular structure is considered an Earth building.

Note of interest: *Most homes built today are square or rectangular shaped, and are built on square or rectangular lots.*

In Feng Shui, the perfect formation of a structure is square (or rectangular) as it "contains" ENERGY.

The element METAL

Radiates to WEST AND NORTHWEST

Season: AUTUMN

Color: WHITE, Gray, Silver, Gold, Soft Pastels, Glittery colors

Element substitution: music, a fan, chimes, bells and other metallic objects

Shapes: Round, CIRCULAR, oval or arched

A structure with a lot of arches and/or soft edges is considered a Metal building.

The element WATER

Radiates to the direction NORTH

Season: WINTER

Colors: Any shade of Blue, Black or Deep Purple

Element substitution: A vase, Fish bowl, fountain, aquarium, glass, mirrors, or cut crystal

Shape: AMORPHOUS like a Lake, River, Pond

An oddly shaped structure where it's difficult to determine the entrance or facing is a Water building.

The element WOOD

Radiates to the directions EAST AND SOUTHEAST

Season: SPRING

Colors: GREEN and the shade of a leaf in any season

Element: TREE, plant, wood floors and furniture, cabinets, bark, leaves

Element substitution: When a tree or plant can't be used, you can use silk plants or flowers or artwork of nature.

Shape: COLUMN or tower

A structure such as a high rise is typically a wood building.

A few TIPS:

To balance an element in an environment, you can add ARTWORK of the element, the color, shape, season or symbol of the element, or a painting representing one of these aspects of the element.

One good piece of artwork in a small room or office environment can balance all five elements.

Don't be afraid to use or wear COLOR in Feng Shui. It is one of the highest vibratory fields of energy on the planet. Even the visually impaired can feel color through their skin.

When an environment radiates to all five elements, your body's energy also radiates to a higher frequency of health as well.

When Feng Shui is done correctly, it nurtures, embraces & supports your visions, dreams, and goals without you even having to think about it.

On the flipside of the coin, when your environment or a real estate listing is out of balance, it will deplete and destroy your (or your client's) energy systems over time.

An "energetically" out-of-balance property does not magnetize the right buyer, highest price and/or an easy transaction.

When a property listing is harmonically in balance, all five elements vibrate together and the environment (effortlessly) attracts a faster SALE, and more times than not with multiple offers to boot.

FOR EXAMPLE:

When the land (or lot) and the house have good Feng Shui, a real estate listing becomes a BILLBOARD ADVERTISEMENT for more listings, sales, and referral business.

OR, if you are a homeowner, your property will act as a MAGNET to attract countless opportunities and blessings.

This is another aspect of the MAGIC AND REALITY of GOOD Feng Shui.

Chapter Eleven

ELEMENTALLY Speaking

Imagine Fire, Earth, Metal, Water, and Wood existing in a constant dynamic of CREATION.

These elements are the primal forces of creation, NOT ONLY in an environment, but in you as well. Each one of these elements is a highly active and creative ingredient in your psyche, in your biology, in your emotions and in your mind.

This is a REALITY of Feng Shui.

Everything you have learned thus far is applicable to the practice of western Feng Shui for your home and office, and to marketing and selling property faster.

However, there is one classical school of Feng Shui that you will want to take advantage of when it comes to:

BUYING AND SELLING PROPERTY

COMMUNICATING AND/OR NEGOTIATING WITH CLIENTS AND RELATIONS

WORKING

SLEEPING

LOVE RELATIONSHIPS

HEALTH

CREATION AND MORE...

If you recall, this classical school was listed as the first MIRACLE of Feng Shui and it IS indeed miraculous.

Again, it's called EIGHT MANSIONS or BA ZHAI Feng Shui.

Because this classical approach/school is a complex study of its own, the most important thing you need to know about it *is that..*

In this classical school of Feng Shui, there are EIGHT CHINESE ELEMENTS, not FIVE, and you are one of the EIGHT...!

There are two types of EARTH people, two types of WOOD people, two types of METAL people and only one type of WATER and FIRE element people.

Once you know who you are "elementally" and how your unique DNA and energy vibrates, you will be able to SUPER CHARGE everything you know and have learned to date about Feng Shui, and use your unique talents to grace your life.

To discover your Feng Shui element, visit

Fengshuibenefits.com/elements

For now – here is a **GENERAL** description of FIRE, EARTH, METAL, WATER, and WOOD element PEOPLE. Please keep in mind that when it comes to Earth, Metal, and Wood element people, it's difficult (at best) to generalize.

FIRE ELEMENT PEOPLE are:

Temperamental and impatient

Not afraid of danger and usually love animals

Quick to get excited about people, places, and things and just as fast to let them go

Nature and sun lovers

Narcissistic at times

Demanding and loud

Into sports physically or as spectators

Bad enemies to have

Travelers of the world

Not loners, and they love to be the center of attention

Inspirational

Alive and impulsive

Prone to heart, eye, circulation, and hand problems

FUN – FUN – FUN people to be with -- when they are happy

EARTH ELEMENT PEOPLE are:

Comfort creatures

Indecisive on what they want to do with their lives

Practical and earthy by nature

Generally, they are multi-talented from business to music to technology to art to you name it.

Procrastinators par excellence

Happy with anything to do with or in nature

Collectors of things and tend to clutter their environment

Usually overweight

Romantic and can make bad judgements in relationships

Easily intimidated by others when they are out of balance

Nurturing, kind and thoughtful people

Prone to spleen, stomach, digestive and muscle problems

Natural healers

METAL ELEMENT PEOPLE are:

Neat and clean and love beautiful environments

People who like to make lists of things to do

Respectful of law, order, and justice

Not happy being controlled or limited – they like their options

Obsessive Compulsive when out of balance

Bright and creative

Very good with money and finances

People who can turn chaos into order

Extremely sensitive to the environment

Prone to lung, head, teeth, and skin problems - basically everything from the lungs up

Honest to a fault

Refined and grateful by nature

WATER ELEMENT PEOPLE are:

Deep thinkers

Emotional and withdrawn at times

People who don't mind repetitive tasks or eating at the same places all the time

Persuasive and dynamic when centered and balanced

Usually very intelligent and creative

People who love the arts or like to act/write/produce

Very honest and loyal

Opposed to change

Feng Shui

Fearful of many things

Collectors of valuable items

Often secretive and mysterious

Loners most of the time, as they live in their heads

Prone to kidney, bladder, blood, lower back, and knee problems

Spiritual and intuitive and sometimes psychic

WOOD ELEMENT PEOPLE are:

Into sweet things like chocolate, candies, and pastries

People with addictions that are hard to knock

Rooted and grounded and can grow plants and businesses

Gentle spirits who are kindhearted until taken advantage of –
then watch out

Refined and cultured – love books, songs, movies, and romance

Educated and don't mind reading and writing documents and
contracts

People who often suffer from low self-esteem and self-worth

Depressed more than the other elements – except for perhaps
earth and water

Stubborn and unyielding when they want their way

Active, driven, and competitive

Prone to liver, tendon, upper back, and bone problems

Loyal and generous

Concerned about humanity

Chapter Twelve

Dress for SUCCESS

Did you know that you can dress for HAPPINESS AND SUCCESS too?

When you are in your element, you automatically feel more peaceful, grounded, and centered. People will comment and tell you that you look great or that you are radiant.

The FIVE ELEMENTS work well in business and relationships as well.

FOR EXAMPLE:

If you are a REALTOR® and you are working with a first-time buyer or you are an adult communicating with a child, you will want to REDUCE your energy so that you do not overwhelm the other person. Refer to THE REDUCTIVE CYCLE of elements and wear the element colors that follows yours in the diagram on chapter SEVEN.

Conversely, if you are a REALTOR® working with a MULTI-MILLION DOLLAR buyer, you will want to increase your energy or vibration by wearing a color in the PRODUCTIVE cycle of elements. The same applies to a life partner who wants to get his/her point across to their mate. Thus, you will want to wear one of the colors of the element that precedes yours in the diagram on chapter SEVEN.

Wearing a tie, a hankie, a scarf, a piece of jewelry or even the right shade of lipstick can do the trick. The goal is to IGNITE or REDUCE the vibration of energy around your FACE, depending on your audience and what you are communicating.

I go into much greater detail on the EIGHT element people in my Feng Shui CERTIFCATION program. In short, it's "extremely important" for people in sales (of any nature) to learn about EAST and WEST GROUP people, and how they process information.

This classical school of Feng Shui is BRILLIANT, and easy to use. Once you know and understand your client's (or children's) element – you will be able to speak to them in a way of which they can - HEAR you.

For REALTORS® and people in sales, you will be able to "communicate and negotiate" in unprecedented ease and speed. This equates to reducing your time, energy, stress level and work load by 50% or more, while providing extraordinary service.

Chapter Thirteen

Core Principle Number THREE

Okay, now.

It's time to relax a bit and take a deep breath.

Ahhhhhhhhhhhh....

As you take the next breath in, gently expel more WIND than you took in on the inhale.

Try again now, and this time, focus on the inhale breath.

As you breathe in, you are experiencing the next force of nature in Feng Shui.

This life force energy you are breathing in and out is called CHI.

CHI IS THE THIRD CORE PRINCIPLE OF SUCCESSFUL FENG SHUI.

What you need to know is that CHI influences REALITY and CREATES MAGIC.

This energy is the interactive essence of the five elements in nature.

The Chinese refer to this essence as CHI (or Qi). I will use the word CHI as you continue to learn about the most powerful life force in nature. In the Western world, we refer to this life force as...ENERGY.

ENERGY is POWERFUL.

It can "stream or scream."

It can be auspicious or destructive... like a gentle soothing, nurturing, life-giving breeze or like a tornado.

CHI is the Cosmic breath of life.

CHI is both visible and invisible.

For example, let's take electricity. We can't visibly see electricity, but we can flip on a switch and see the evidence of its presence. Likewise, we can't see wind, but we can feel it blowing through our hair or see it blowing the leaves on a tree.

Gravity is another example of the INVISIBLE life force energy referred to as CHI.

About this Life Force.

Matter is considered VISIBLE energy. Everything in your environment that you can visibly see is matter. Matter is dense energy and vibrates slowly, which enables you to see it.

CHI is a baby's cry at birth.

It is the power behind crashing waves on the shore.

A flower's fragrance and bloom is full of CHI.

CHI is not exclusive to the Chinese culture. Every culture has CHI.

They just refer to it by a different name.

For example:

The Japanese refer to it as KI.

The Greeks refer to it as PNEUMA.

The Egyptians refer to it a ANKH.

The Hindus: PRANA

Hebrews: RAH (Raw)

Even the Catholics refer to it as SPIRITUS.

To manifest powerful results with Feng Shui, the flow and accumulation of positive life force ENERGY MUST BE TOP PRIORITY.

Whether you use it to:

❖ Remedy and enhance a difficult to sell property or listing

❖ Set the intention to increase your business 100% in 6 months

❖ Design your dream home

❖ Create harmony & balance in your home or garden

EVERYTHING YOU DO IN LIFE IS DEPENDENT ON CHI

Thus, it's extremely important to capitalize on it, no matter what it is you wish to Feng Shui or manifest in your life.

Again, to manifest powerful results with Feng Shui, the flow and accumulation of positive life force ENERGY must be top priority.

Whether the elements are visible or invisible doesn't matter; what matters is that this life force flows through all things - through buildings, people, mountains, rivers, power lines and even parking lots.

So, when CHI is POSITIVE, it supports, nurtures, and enriches your life and career.

When it is SHA, (not positive), it will diminish, deplete and destroy your energy systems over time.

When CHI becomes chaotic, fast, stagnant, stuck, or dangerous, like a poison arrow, it is SHA.

When you Feng Shui, you will want to focus your ATTENTION on the "accumulation" of POSITIVE Life Force ENERGY ONLY.

CHI = ENERGY

- EVERYTHING IS... **ALIVE**
- EVERYTHING IS... **CONNECTED**
- EVERYTHING IS... **CHANGING**
- EVERYTHING IS... **DYNAMIC**
- EVERYTHING... **CYCLES**
- EVERYTHING... **RADIATES**
- EVERYTHING... **ATTRACTS**
- EVERYTHING... **MAGNETIZES**
- EVERYTHING IN THE UNIVERSE IS... **ENERGY**

CHI is the Life Force in every single living and non-living thing on planet earth.

It is both Spirit and Matter.

CHI – (ENERGY) - is the central concept to raising or increasing the vibration in Feng Shui.

I've been asked many times: "Is all CHI the same?"

The answer is NO.

Good CHI is easy to recognize. It flows smoothly, effortlessly, and gently.

It likes to meander like a stream. This is the type of CHI you want to accumulate in your home and work space, because it is what supports and nurtures your life, career, and MOTHER EARTH.

SHA CHI, or chaotic, stagnant, stuck, heavy, or destructive CHI, will deplete and destroy your energy and wreak havoc on your life.

Because we live in a holographic universe, YOU are your environment, whether it be your home, office, briefcase, or car. You are reflected in everything.

When your environment is free of clutter, your life and mind will become more gentle and free of clutter and anxiety as well.

When your CHI is chaotic or stuck, your life will mirror the same energy. Therefore, everything in your environment is continuously dictating the quality of your life.

Why does LESS MEAN MORE in Feng Shui?

Less means more INNER CHI.

More Energy.

It's an interesting phenomenon to work hard all your life to accumulate things, then to realize one day that less actually brings you MORE peace, joy, and harmony.

Everything on your land, and everything in your home and office, and even on your desk, is but a metaphor for what is going on in your life – at any point in time.

It's important not to forget that Feng Shui is an earthly art and science.

After many years of teaching and consulting, I've come to learn that the "environment" is more valuable than the land you own - and the land you own is more important than the house (building/structure) you occupy.

The structure, or your home, is more valuable than the rooms you live and work in, and the rooms are more important than YOU.

Now you might be asking yourself: – "How can this possibly be true?" OR you're probably wondering why the Chinese would value land more than people?

THE ANSWER IS SIMPLE:

In the Asian culture, a blade of grass is an integral part of the whole. The Chinese do not see themselves separate from nature; they see themselves as ONE with nature.

They believe that if your environment is beautiful, it will take care of your land, and the land will take care of your house, and the house will take care of the rooms inside.

Therefore, if the rooms inside are ELEMENTALLY AND ENERGETICALLY in balance, everyone will automatically be healthy, balanced and blessed.

In Feng Shui, there is no separation between a blade of grass and the building or the home you occupy. Likewise, there is no separation between you and I.

Today, Feng Shui is used to regulate and control the flow of CHI – ENERGY - in all work and living environments, including landscapes.

Architecture, building design, configuration, orientation, the placement of furniture, and the relationship of Yin/Yang and the FIVE elements all affect the way CHI flows in and out and around your life.

The West can learn from the East!

I doubt that you have ever gone to the home of an Asian family without seeing a beautiful garden. This is because they know that if they care for the land (their gardens), nature will care for their lives.

In our Western culture, most people see themselves as separate from nature. Yet, until you recognize the ONENESS of everything - you as humanity, you as a blade of grass, you as your home, you as your office, you as your desk and you & me as ONE - you will not know the INFINITE JOY AND BLISS that you divinely and rightfully deserve.

SO, if you learn only one thing of value reading this book, only one principle of Feng Shui, my wish for you is to comprehend and appreciate the awesome POWER OF CHI - ENERGY.

For CHI is everywhere and in everything.

It cannot be destroyed.

However, via Feng Shui, it can be skillfully controlled and directed to create PEACE, HARMONY, AND BALANCE.

Thus, when CHI is alive and vibrant, it becomes a beacon and a magnet for all your dreams, goals, and intentions to manifest effortlessly, from selling a house to creating a power station at work, or sacred space in your home or garden.

Given this, if you are open to embracing a new perspective on WHO AND WHAT YOU ARE, then hopefully you will see....

THAT YOU ARE PURE AND INFINITE CHI..ENERGY.

Chapter Fourteen

TIPS on Integrating Feng Shui

If it could be summed up in a sentence, Feng Shui is the CREATION of an optimal environment in which to thrive.

Even if the traditional or classical schools of Feng Shui are a little "out there" for you, modern or western Feng Shui is still a great way for you to design SPACE so that it supports and empowers you.

To fully integrate Feng Shui into your home and work place, you will want to practice the THREE CORE PRINCIPLES wherever you go.

This means recognizing that you, the people you know (including your clients), and all the circumstances of your life and those of others are nothing more than reflections of the SPACE and environment in which you or they occupy.

This TRUTH is a powerful concept that will allow you to increase the effectiveness of Feng Shui in your life.

To this end, here are a few steps you can take right away to integrate Feng Shui in your home, office, and/or real estate listings:

DE-CLUTTER AND ORGANIZE THE ENVIRONMENT

- Clutter and disorganization in your environment is simply not compatible with good Feng Shui.

- Clearing (all) clutter and organizing your environment is the first step to integrating Feng Shui into your lifestyle.

- Clutter impedes the flow of energy and makes good Feng Shui impossible.

- Clutter includes anything and everything from dirty dishes to toys lying around the house, to dirty clothes needing to be thrown in the washing machine, to stacks of files and/or 'stuff' lying around that have no purpose or usefulness.

- SPACE CLEARING is one of the most rejuvenating and rewarding steps that you can take for yourself and those you love, so make it a POSITIVE (not a negative) experience.

- Clearing SPACE will open you up to a new sense of clarity and feeling of well-being.

- GIFT AWAY special items and belongings to your children and friends while you are alive. If not, you will never be able to see the surprise and joy in the eyes and faces of your beloved receivers.

- A good tip to follow when getting rid of "stuff" is to examine each item and ask yourself if you should give it away, store it, or throw it away.

PLANTS AND FLOWERS ENRICH THE ENVIRONMENT

- Plants are truly wonderful in Feng Shui because they are not only symbolic of nature, but they are "life force" energy itself.

- You can never have too many FLOWERS in your home, but you can have too many plants (the wood element), so be careful.

- Placing plants near electrical outlets and electronic equipment, such as TVs, computers, and other electrical devices (even microwaves), will help to absorb SHA CHI, or electrical magnetic energy that is harmful to your health.

- Finally, remember to keep each of your plants watered, exposed to enough sunlight, and keep them green and healthy. If plants in your environment look dead or dying, make sure to remove them immediately.

- Remember that you are your environment.

TOILETS AND DRAINS DEPLETE ENERGY IN THE ENVIRONMENT

- Water is huge in Feng Shui, as it is one of the five natural elements; however, toilets and drains need to be covered when not in use, as they take energy away from your home.

- The mere symbolism of water being flushed down the drain can have a negative effect on your health and finances, which is why you will want to keep your toilet lid down to minimize any negative effects.

- **NOTE:** There are exceptions to the above when integrating classical Feng Shui techniques and remedies to properties.

TOSS OUT ANY NEGATIVE IMAGERY IN THE ENVIRONMENT

- This step is the most personal for you, because only you can decide what is negative imagery or what brings negative images to your mind.

- Strangely enough, one item could be a laptop that symbolizes work that you don't enjoy doing. If so, it's wise to keep your laptop at the office and keep your home computer free.

- So, look around your home for any décor items or symbols that bring negative emotions or thoughts to your mind. This can be anything from greeting cards, emails, photos and/or gifts from past relationships that were not safe, healthy, or ended badly for you.

- It can also be furniture you inherited and don't like. Again, you must be honest with yourself and remove all "emotionally charged" belongings from your environment to help you create peace and harmony in your life.

- Keep items that nurture and support you; however, only keep them if they do not clutter your environment.

- In Feng Shui, LESS IS MORE. This is because Feng Shui is basically a minimalistic art and science.

THE FLOW OF WATER IN THE ENVIRONMENT

- It's relevant to mention again that WATER is an important element of Feng Shui.

- While the symbolism of a toilet flushing water down the drain is bad Feng Shui and sucks CHI away, the flow of water inside your home or office will "enhance" your life.

- Therefore, you will want to consider adding a fountain or two in your dwelling space.

- An alternative to a fountain would be a fish habitat (no Beta fighting fish) or an aquarium. Eight fish represents present money, and NINE fish (including one black one) represents future wealth and abundance.

- If running (moving) water is not an option in your space, it is perfectly fine for you to place a bowl or two of floating flowers or candles or vases of water with flowers in them (even silk ones will do). The important consideration is to have "visible" WATER inside your home.

SUNLIGHT – YANG ENERGY IN THE ENVIRONMENT

- An element of nature that has more positive energy than water is the SUN, and it is free.

- A home that is closed off from the sun or doesn't allow sunlight in is simply not compatible with a good Feng Shui lifestyle.

- All windows should be exposed to sunlight.

- Sunlight is symbolic of many things, including motivation, productivity, optimal health, along with the prospects of a more active love life.

- While it's ok to keep your blinds or window coverings closed at night, you will want to make it a habit to open them in the morning.

- Because we have become reliant on lighting produced from electricity, we have unintentionally forgotten about the natural source of sunlight that is universal to us all.

- The sun NUTURES and EMPOWERS us in countless ways.

THE USE OF COLOR IN THE ENVIRONMENT

When you Feng Shui, don't be afraid to use COLOR. Color is a high vibratory field of energy that ATTRACTS blessings, friendly relations, fun and good fortune.

However, the reverse is also true. Make sure not to fall into the "pretty" trap, and fail to honor the basic principles of THE FIVE ELEMENTS.

The over dominant use of one or two colors (elements) inside a room or environment can wreak havoc on one's HEALTH and

FINANCES, especially if the occupant's "personal" Feng Shui Element is not compatible with the color(s) used in the environment.

SPACE EQUALS THE ENVIRONMENT

Sensual and Sacred SPACE epitomizes good Feng Shui.

All the rooms in your home deserve harmonious energy— especially your bedroom. With its impact on sleep quality and well-being, the design of your bedroom should not be neglected.

If you want your bedroom to be a restful retreat, Feng Shui can help.

If ROMANCE is important to you, the master bedroom should exude *Sensuality, Sexuality, and Sacredness.*

Kitty litter boxes, computers, TVs, clothes on the floor and clutter do not support an intimate communion.

Here are 20 tips to improving LOVE AND ROMANCE in the Bedroom: Fengshuibenefits.com/bedroom

A FEW FENG SHUI LANDSCAPE TIPS

Again, WATER equates to "good" Feng Shui in the garden.

You can bring water in via swimming pools, hot tubs, fountains, ponds, bird baths and/or water walls and falls. Water walls and water falls should flow towards your house.

Wind chimes belong outside, not inside you house. Wind chimes help to circulate stuck energy and/or slow down chaotic energy – SHA CHI. They are best placed on corner eves.

Add motion to your garden with colorful spinners, flags, moving sculptures, mobiles, wind socks and/or whirly gigs to keep energy moving.

CHI on the ground likes to meander.

It's important to have "undulating lines" in your landscape to slow down energy so that it can embrace your life. Therefore, kidney-shaped flower beds and meandering pathways not only slow down energy, but they also enhance the odds of good fortune and blessings coming into your life.

COLOR radiates energy, and each color has its own unique vibration. You can never have enough color in your GARDEN, but you can overdo color inside your home or office and suffer. All 5 elements must be in harmony and balance in your living and work environments. (Refer to the PRODUCTIVE CYCLE of the five elements.)

Learn more about the benefits of color in your garden at:

Fengshuibenefits.com/garden

You can use my (free) **ENERGY BLUEPRINT** when arranging color and/or the symbols of color in your landscape or garden. Click below to receive it.

Fengshuibenefits.com/bagua

Chapter Fifteen

Your True Life's PURPOSE

We have covered a lot of territory discussing "just" THREE PRINCIPLES of Feng Shui.

-YIN/YANG

-THE FIVE CHINESE ELEMENTS

-THE POWER OF CHI

These core principles set the GROUND WORK, the FOUNDATION, for "good" Feng Shui.

When properly INTEGRATED, blessings and miracles start to become everyday occurrences. However, the most phenomenal GIFT of Feng Shui is that it supports and empowers you to find...

YOUR TRUE LIFE'S PURPOSE.

It's my belief that we each come into the world with a LIFE PURPOSE...to share with others.

We recognize it because it is a gift that deeply fulfills us. It's a talent that is uniquely our own. It also fully expresses the core "essence" of our SPIRIT... who we are and why we are here.

The old paradigm of pursuing a career or working "solely" to acquire riches and security depletes our "life force"... ENERGY.

Unfortunately, more than 80% of humanity still has not learned this lesson yet, resulting in people staying "stuck" in heartache, anxiety, struggle, and stress, while continuing to believe that money will erase their deepest fears, problems, and pain.

Einstein said: "The significant problems we face cannot be solved at the same level of thinking we were at when we created them."

He also implied that insanity is doing the same thing over and over again and expecting a different outcome.

Feng Shui is the CHANGE AGENT of a new paradigm.

Via Feng Shui, I believe that we are each worthy of GREATNESS when we are "authentically" in our GIFT, and when we are not, we sacrifice both our self-worth and self-esteem.

It is at this point of "imbalance" that we not only risk continuous heartache but also experience physical and spiritual depletion.

In your darkest hour, it takes "fearless faith and great courage" to TRUST in God, or the omnipresence, as the "source" of your fulfillment.

Paradoxically, not until you are in alignment with this truth can you experience your greatness or your gift.

With Respect to Feng Shui.

Without peace, harmony and balance in your home and workplace, you cannot begin to "grasp" the DIVINE that is forever present in your life.

Equally, being surrounded by mayhem makes it difficult to trust that the path (your life purpose) will appear and support you in rich and abundant ways.

Herein lies my GIFT.

The ability to take you from 3D reality to higher realms of consciousness, so that your life's PURPOSE manifests on time, and so that you can share the INFINITE BEING that you truly are ... with all of humanity.

It is in this state of GRACE that you become ONE with Time, Space, People, and the Earth, and begin to TRUST that everything that "is or isn't" happening in your life is for your highest good and evolution.

A balanced environment also supports you in LETTING GO OF FEAR.

All life breathes together. It takes a conscious, focused effort to live life without fear or defensiveness.

Feng Shui provides the "energetic field" of protection, the preference and wisdom for you to step outside the box of the mundane and TRUST IN YOURSELF.

When fear is absent, you will automatically experience the infinite "divine intelligence" operating in, as and through you...*effortlessly.*

It is in this moment of the MIRACULOUS that you will begin to understand the ancient Chinese proverb:

"That a bird does not sing because it has an answer, it sings because it has a SONG."

I hope that you have enjoyed *The MYTH, MAGIC and REALITY of Feng Shui,* and that you will practice the THREE CORE PRINCIPLES as a way of life.

If you do, you will experience an INNER PEACE AND POWER beyond your wildest vision and dreams, and you will awaken to your true life's purpose and bliss.

BLESS YOU ON YOUR FENG SHUI JOURNEY.

May YOU Delight the World with Compassion, Kindness, Balance, and Your TRUE Self.

Suzee Miller

ABOUT THE AUTHOR

Suzee Miller

Feng Shui Author • Educator • Consultant

Suzee Miller has been active in Business, Feng Shui and Real Estate for over three decades. She helped to open the first two RE/MAX franchises in the state of California over 30 years ago.

As a successful entrepreneur, Ms. Miller's accomplishments have been published in Who's Who In Business in California, and Who's Who of Women in Real Estate in the United States.

She is a graduate of the American Feng Shui Institute, the Lotus Institute of Feng Shui, Grand Master Yap Cheng Hai's Feng Shui Center of Excellence in Malaysia and Grand Master Mantak Chia's Universal Healing Tao Center of Thailand.

In addition, Suzee has studied with famous Tai Chi, Qi Gong and Feng Shui Masters from all over the world to acquire "traditional and contemporary" wisdom and knowledge of the Asian Arts.

Bridging the gap between classical Feng Shui and contemporary Feng Shui, and between metaphysics and quantum physics, Suzee has become the Leader in the industry - introducing INTEGRATIVE Feng Shui to individuals and real estate professionals worldwide.

Suzee Miller is also the Creator of *The INTERNATIONAL FENG SHUI CERTIFICATION.* Feng Shui Certification is available to architects, builders, developers, designers/decorators, stagers, city planners, space planners, homeowners, real estate professionals, Feng Shui practitioners and individuals who are interested in MASTERING integrative Feng Shui.

Her self-study program is designed to learn at your own pace. CERTIFICATION can be taken for personal or professional advancement, or for educational purposes only.

Suzee believes that:

"Every HOMEBUYER, RENTER AND REAL ESTATE PROFESSIONAL needs to be educated on the differences between "good and bad" lots, locations, houses and floor plans "before" renting or buying property.

If you are a real estate agent, it's important to know this information PRIOR TO showing a BUYER property.

Only INTEGRATIVE Feng Shui addresses the power of the "seen and unseen" ENERGIES that occupy SPACE and that affect us in small and large ways.

It's important to UNDERSTAND that these energies can either deplete and destroy one's health, finances and reputation, or enhance and enrich one's wealth, reputation and body temple."

BONUS CHAPTER

The ORIGIN And Reality Of Feng Shui

Feng Shui has its early origins thousands of years ago in China.

It began when people first began to settle in China to raise livestock and grow crops.

Back then, Feng Shui was used to select homes that would be safe and flourishing for families. Later, Feng Shui was further applied to identify safe places for monuments, government buildings, and even cities.

Feng Shui grew to be a more essential part of Chinese culture and eventually evolved into a more intricate observation of both the man-made and natural environment in general, and specifically on how the energy of the earth affects different places and the people living in those places.

While Feng Shui did officially originate in China, it would be unfair not to mention that India had a role in its origins as well. This is because there is archeological evidence that Indian mystics practiced forms of Feng Shui between five to six thousand years ago.

Just like the Chinese, Indians used Feng Shui to select places to build homes, governmental buildings/palaces, and cities. There is also substantial evidence that over three thousand years ago, Indian monks crossed through Tibet in northern India and into Southwestern China.

The Chinese also adopted some of the practices that the Indians had developed, called '**Vastu Shastra** (vāstu śāstra).' These principles were then further developed into more schools of Feng Shui, some of which are variations of different schools of Feng Shui that are known today.

Feng Shui has never remained static.

The more this study has evolved and developed over time, the more we have learned.

Ancient Asian civilizations such as China and India originally used the core principles to select burial sites and homes for nomadic people, before expanding the principles to design and layout of their cities. In fact, many prominent Asian cities today were founded completely on the principles of Feng Shui, including the capital of China.

Feng Shui in Asia

Feng Shui was never recorded in history until the last century. The elder Feng Shui masters of ancient times would teach Feng Shui from Master to Pupil. Only spoken teachings by word of mouth were learned.

It was prohibited to speak of Feng Shui, because at various times in history, it was considered superstition or the occult. The Feng Shui Master would learn verses, quatrains, and poems and recite them to his pupils so it was not recorded. This was done to not endanger lives.

Surprisingly, today, many young Chinese do not know about Feng Shui, and many who do know about it do not believe in it. Also, some Asians believe in the principles of Feng Shui but do not realize that they are an integral part of Feng Shui.

There is also a group of Chinese/Asians who do not believe in Feng Shui because they mistakenly believe it opposes religion. This is one of the many MYTHS of Feng Shui, as Feng Shui is the study of ENERGY, and energy does not oppose religion.

Feng Shui in the Western World Today

Feng Shui is no longer exclusively a Chinese art and science. Feng Shui is now taking roots internationally. The Western world, and all cultures of the world, are now embracing Feng Shui as a way of life.

Today, Westerners outnumber Asians TEN TO ONE in embracing and integrating Feng Shui principles into their lives.

For most of its history, Feng Shui remained absent from Western civilization. That changed in the 1980s when interest in Feng Shui in the United States began to grow. Today, Western interest in Feng Shui has expanded across North America, Australia, South America, and Europe.

Years ago, in discussion with one of my Chinese Masters (teachers), I was told: *"China brought Feng Shui to America, but America will take Feng Shui to a whole new level."*

I asked him why he felt this way, and he replied:

"In China, if a Chinese Master says to move a door ONE foot, the client will move it even if the cost to do so is more than $100,000. The reason being, he stated, is that the Chinese do not QUESTION a Master, whereas in America – people question everything!"

This is true. I have witnessed it in my Feng Shui career. The evolution of this art and science has been phenomenal to experience.

So, even though WIND AND WATER (Feng Shui) may seem like a foreign concept, the TRUTH is that as a human being you are... 100% FENG SHUI.

This is a REALITY.

For more than 60% of your adult body is WATER, and according to H.H. Mitchell, Journal of Biological Chemistry 158, the brain and heart are composed of **73%** water, and the lungs are about 83% WATER.

Thus, without WATER, you would die in a matter of days, and without WIND (air), you would die within minutes.

Herein lies the reasons why the core principles of Feng Shui need to be understood (completely) and integrated properly in your home and investment properties. It insures that your environment will support your most precious gift – **your body temple.**

Classical and western approaches of Feng Shui come down to the same truth.

The more you live in harmony with your environment, the happier, healthier, and more personally fulfilled you will be. This is a concept that transcends geographical locations and cultures, and is beneficial to anyone who decides to utilize Feng Shui.

This said, the western schools of Feng Shui can be perceived as different from the more classical schools of Feng Shui.

Classical Feng Shui has traditionally been used to determine how to place a building or a city on land. It takes into consideration numerous factors which include the observation of land, a repeatable and complex math calculation, methodologies based on physical forces in the universe and on time cycles in the SOLAR system that affect both people and space.

In contrast to this, the western schools of Feng Shui put less of an emphasis on the literal placement of buildings and a stronger emphasis on positive living. In other words, the eastern cultural aspects of Feng Shui are largely left out in the western schools.

Then, as if the differences between the EAST AND WEST are not enough for you to grasp, along comes the "customs and superstitions" of the Chinese people to confuse you even more!

FOR EXAMPLE:

RED is often used for the front door, according to Chinese customs, whereas in most classical schools of Feng Shui, the color of an entrance door is determined by its "facing" direction and the unseen energy located there.

Again, altogether different is the western approach to Feng Shui that recommends using whatever color you personally enjoy the most in order to enhance your positive feelings as much as possible. According to western Feng Shui, this will lift your personal CHI more than RED or a color determined by direction, particularly if you have a dislike for red or another color!

Feng Shui, as it is taught in the western world, also puts more of an emphasis on practicality and cultural considerations instead of on "positive vs. negative" - or the UNSEEN OR INVISIBLE energy. This is because something that is perceived as being negative in one culture may instead be perceived as the opposite or positive in another culture.

FOR EXAMPLE:

In the United States, the number '13' (especially on a Friday) has a very negative connotation to it and is often associated with bad luck, death, or misfortune.
Likewise, in China, the number '4' has a negative connotation to it as it sounds like the word "death" in the Chinese language.

Having Americans or Westerners, in general, avoiding the use of the number four would not make much sense because it's purely a Chinese superstition.

In a visa versa scenario, it wouldn't make sense for people who are Chinese to avoid the use of the number 13. Nonetheless, regardless of your culture or orientation, if you believe a number is "negative," then IT IS, and you will want to avoid renting or buying a home with the number in it.

So, while traditional or classical schools of Feng Shui and the more modern or western schools of Feng Shui may have their differences, they also have their similarities.

A major teaching of Feng Shui "in general" is that small things or small spaces impact us in large ways.

Think of it this way. When water drips against a rock, it doesn't appear to do anything. However, over the course of time, the water will slowly erode the rock. While small things like the water dripping in your home may seem like nothing, over time, it will affect your energy.

Examples of seemingly small things that lower or weaken your energy include objects or colors that have negative connotations, weapons or objects that can be used as weapons to injure people, artwork that conveys a negative message, or disorganization and clutter.

In fact, "clutter" is one of the biggest threats to positive living.

There are other small things that may be unique to your own personal beliefs that are positive or negative. This becomes a very important consideration!

FOR EXAMPLE:

If you have a piece of furniture from a previous relationship that went poorly, it may remind you of a negative part of your life, and therefore, it is not a positive article in your environment.

Even though a sofa is neither negative or positive, and it may be positive for other people, for you, it's negative and needs to be replaced– if the above applies.

This is just one instance of how Feng Shui can be unique to you in a personal way.

In short, both classical Feng Shui as it has traditionally been practiced in eastern Asia and western Feng Shui as it is being practiced now in North America and Europe have their differences and similarities.

But in the end, it all comes down to clearing your home of objects that bring you down and replacing them with objects that evoke positive emotions that lift your spirit, your ENERGY.

It's also important to include objects or décor items of nature and/or which inspire you.

While your home does not need to look perfect, it does have to accurately reflect your essence and personal taste. It also needs to be organized and clutter free, with no colors or objects present that upset your emotions or that hinder the quality of your life.

The MYTH that Feng Shui is about superstition is simply that: a MYTH.

Case in point, hanging wind chimes inside your home hoping they will bring you good fortune has nothing to do with Feng Shui. It is strictly a Chinese belief.

Feng Shui is about learning how to focus and direct energy in your environment and living space to benefit you as optimally as possible and, as a result, to enable you to live a happier, healthier, and more EXPANSIVE life.

So, even though classical Feng Shui and western Feng Shui schools as you may know them have their differences, their similarities are still strong and together they forge the heart of what Feng Shui is today.

A Few Client

TESTIMONIALS

"Suzee presented two of her Feng Shui seminar topics at our WAR state convention. Close to 400 REALTORS® (with standing room only) attended each of her seminars. She was by far the hit of the convention; she literally had to be escorted by monitors to the restroom, as the agents swarmed all over her during the break. The information she presented was well-organized, informative, and unique. Not only that, but she also gracefully combined humor with logic and took a foreign topic and made it exciting and easy to comprehend. We highly recommend Suzee Miller and her seminars on Feng Shui."

Steve Francks, / Executive Vice President, Washington State Association of REALTORS®

"We listened to your Feng Shui Empowerment program last Friday, and went out 2 days later and Feng Shui'd our Sunday open house (a listing on the market over 40 days). It took us less than 30 minutes to Feng Shui it, and to our shock and amazement, within one hour, the first buyer who walked in...bought it!!! The buyer commented: 'this house feels good.' Not only did our seller receive top dollar, but the buyer also put more than 35% down, and we're closing escrow in 30 days! Thank you, Suzee Miller; your Feng Shui techniques are incredible!!!"

Nancy and Mike Fenn, /WCR Members

"I'm the element Mother Earth. Your Feng Shui audio programs are phenomenal. I am only halfway through them, but already the opportunities that are coming along are just UNIMAGINABLE! Thank you."

Manoj Shiynani – Business Entrepreneur/Spain

"Hi, Suzee. I just wanted to take a minute to thank you, thank you for your unbelievable assistance in the sale of our client's home on Ximeno Avenue. Before I convinced my partner that we needed to think outside the box to sell this property, it sat on the market for over two months. We couldn't figure out what to do until we took your advice and Feng Shuied it. It took us less than one hour, and it sold in less than 3 days!!! Today, we Feng Shui all of our listings before putting them into MLS. Thanks, Suzee, for making this fun marketing technique available to us; we're having a dynamic year!"

Francoise Pichon, GRI, CRS/ Keller Williams Real Estate

"I just want to thank Feng Shui & you. It has CHANGED MY LIFE! God bless you. In the country that I live in, we don't have any good resources for Feng Shui education, but now I've found you to share with me all your Feng Shui knowledge. Thank you!"

Catherine Spiridonoff/ Iran

"Suzee, your Feng Shui Certification is the best approach to selling real estate that I have ever taken. I have found new energy! Since I sold the two properties that got me certified, I have Feng Shui'd two more homes... one just sold in 10 days! The seller is singing my praises and wants me to help her find another home to renovate with Feng Shui! Your program changes lives and works in any market. I cannot thank you enough!"

Elwynn Schwartz, Feng Shui Certified REALTOR®, Chattanooga Real Estate Consultants/Tennessee

"Suzee's Feng Shui expertise helped me create form, function, and flow in my office. It has greatly contributed to my peace of mind as well. Our usage of the

five elements has helped me grow my business to be in the TOP 1% in the lending industry. I am grateful to Suzee for sharing her Feng Shui expertise."

Steven Saucer – Loan Officer /CA

"Thank you for all your help on our home. My sleep Apnea is much improved since integrating your Feng Shui techniques. I'm sleeping so much better since sleeping in my best health and sleep position. Feng Shui is AMAZING, and I am very grateful.

Gleyn Reynolds – Homeowner

Hello, Suzee. I am very happy to tell you that I received my order yesterday. I am starting my Feng Shui Certification course now. I'm very excited to be a part of your Feng Shui school. I listened to two audio programs already, and I'm very excited to do the course! I was so happy that you have an easy payment plan so that I can afford it. Thank you very much. God bless."

Myrna Lovett – Homeowner/Japan

"If your certification was a car, it would be a LEXUS or MERCEDES! Thank you for your wisdom and knowledge Suzee. I've read many books on Feng Shui, but your teaching is over-the-top fantastic! I'm thrilled and humbled to be helping people fulfill their dreams, thanks to you."

Janet Sandquist -- Feng Shui Certified Consultant

Suzee Miller may not be Chinese, but I am, and since learning how to Feng Shui my office, I have increased my staff by 20 new people (now 70 employees strong).

Also, since honoring my power directions, it has enabled me to work smarter (4 days/wk – soon to be 3) at work, while tripling my company earnings in one year!!!

Thanks to Suzee, my company is now branded a success!"

Sherri Tong – CEO/Owner, Intergro Health Services

"Thank you so very much Suzee for the wonderful Feng Shui consultation yesterday! Not only were you articulate and knowledgeable, but most empathetic – and what amazed me the most was how you pinpointed my exact problems. I never attributed them to my property, and it took years for me to realize what I was unwittingly doing to my balance...

Jane Adams, PA

"I am listening to your Feng Shui course. and it is wonderful. I have been a Feng Shui Consultant since May of 1999 through the Pyramid School, but I can't believe all the new things I am learning!"

Laleah Pierce, Feng Shui Consultant, FL

"I was literally down to my last few dollars when my sister told me about Suzee Miller. I immediately got on her website and started devouring as much information as I possibly could. I downloaded my Feng Shui element audio and began implementing EVERYTHING Suzee recommended. Within 24 hrs. -- I kid you not -- I pulled in new paying work, a huge new client, I received money from some orders and I finally felt joy & optimism again. My creativity is renewed, and I have a revived outlook on my life. Thank you, Suzee, for all your brilliance and Feng Shui mastery."

Carine Horner, Artist, Musician, Graphic Designer

A Comment from a Feng Shui CERTIFIED REALTOR®

"Thanks for everything, Suzee; you are a fabulous educator. I've learned so much from your Feng Shui Certification.

For those of you reading my testimonial and success with Feng Shui, this is what I would like you to know from my heart to your heart and home. No matter what you do in life, DON'T sit around waiting for life to happen or for your career to improve when you can be IN the money, having the lifestyle you deserve NOW.

Suzee Miller is a Master who specializes in real estate and WEALTH Feng Shui!

Additionally, if you are a homebuyer or renter, make sure you learn what good and bad Feng Shui lots, locations, houses, and rooms look like "before" making a move. Like me, you will thank Suzee every day of your life that you did!"

Here is my most recent, UNBELIEVABLE but True SUCCESS story!

Feng Shui helped me sell my home in 4 days with only ONE OFFER, last month!

Not only that, but I got $11,000 over the asking price for it as well!!!

Bless you, Suzee, for teaching me Feng Shui in real estate. It has changed my life and destiny forever."

JoAnn VISAretis
SSR, ABR
Feng Shui Certified
RE/MAX JAZZ Inc., Brokerage
CANADA

To view Feng Shui SUCCESS STORIES by category, visit:

Fengshuibenefits.com/success

For Feng Shui Products, visit:

Fengshuibenefits.com/education

To inquire about a Feng Shui Consultation, visit:

Fengshuibenefits.com/contact

To learn how to identify good lots, locations, houses, floor plans, and "how to" Feng Shui correctly from A to Z, visit:

Fengshuibenefits.com/certification

References:

Fengshuibenefits.com/references

Follow Suzee On Facebook: @SuzeeMillerFengShui

In appreciation for embracing Feng Shui principles in your life, input code Suzee at check-out and SAVE 20% on my Feng Shui Products.

89009794R00064

Made in the USA
Lexington, KY
21 May 2018